The DARKNESS and the STARS

The DARKNESS and the STARS

A Story of Loss and Hope

Dawn Anderson

Copyright © 2022 Dawn Anderson.

All rights reserved. No part of this book may be used or reproduced by any means, graphic, electronic, or mechanical, including photocopying, recording, taping or by any information storage retrieval system without the written permission of the author except in the case of brief quotations embodied in critical articles and reviews.

This book is a work of non-fiction. Unless otherwise noted, the author and the publisher make no explicit guarantees as to the accuracy of the information contained in this book and in some cases, names of people and places have been altered to protect their privacy.

Archway Publishing books may be ordered through booksellers or by contacting:

Archway Publishing
1663 Liberty Drive
Bloomington, IN 47403
www.archwaypublishing.com
844-669-3957

Because of the dynamic nature of the Internet, any web addresses or links contained in this book may have changed since publication and may no longer be valid. The views expressed in this work are solely those of the author and do not necessarily reflect the views of the publisher, and the publisher hereby disclaims any responsibility for them.

Any people depicted in stock imagery provided by Getty Images are models, and such images are being used for illustrative purposes only. Certain stock imagery © Getty Images.

ISBN: 978-1-6657-2752-5 (sc)
ISBN: 978-1-6657-2751-8 (hc)
ISBN: 978-1-6657-2753-2 (e)

Library of Congress Control Number: 2022913986

Print information available on the last page.

Archway Publishing rev. date: 10/12/2022

For Mike. Forever the brightest star.

I have loved the stars too fondly to be fearful of the night.
—*Sarah Williams*

CONTENTS

Foreword xi
Introduction xiii
The Backstory 1
The Accident 5
The Aftermath 15
The Nuclear Winter 31
    Can't Compute 32
        The Visions 33
        The Pain 36
    God 39
    Africa 42
Reflections on Grief 49
    The Things People Say 49
    Fire and Ash 52

Loneliness...54

Memories 55

Homesick..58

Ridiculous...59

Panic..59

Devastation..60

Grieving Two Things..61

Sole Keeper of the Memories..................................65

Photographs...66

The Fallout 67

The Dreams 68

Coping..72

**The Gifts: *A Conclusion and a Continuation
of Grief*** 81

FOREWORD

The first time I met Dawn Anderson, I knew she was a deep well of beauty and knowledge and that she had a book in her. Her heart overflows into this work of truth, vulnerability, and art, breathing experience and breath into the parts of being human we don't always speak of.

Dawn infuses softness, mystery, questions, love, and death into her moving story of crushing loss—a story we as people will all experience in our own lives in different forms. This book is a healing journey—medicine and acceptance for the grieving soul, and hope for the weary.

Victoria Erickson
Author, *Rhythms and Roads*

INTRODUCTION

What do you do when the unthinkable happens? What do you do when your whole world comes crashing down all around you? What do you do when the most impossible, most unacceptable, most devastating thing occurs? What do you do when it happens to *you*?

Well. It happened to me. And this is my story.

The underlying premise of my story is as old as time. Tragedy. Loss. Grief.

I'm certainly not the first person in the world who has experienced great loss, and I won't be the last. There is plenty of all that in the world. I am also not the first person to write about it. In fact, I've been humbled and inspired by the many talented writers who have lost loved ones before me, and who have shared *their* stories. Martha Whitmore Hickman, Michelle Steinke-Baumgard, Nora McInerny, and Anne Lamott, among so many other brilliant writers, are my true heroes. I marvel at their use of words and how they can harness the intangible and make it real for the rest of us. I sit in awe at their skill, as before me they weave a complex tapestry of human emotions from sheer words, nuanced and deep, and I celebrate how they give my mind a foothold on the slippery cliff of understanding what the hell happened to *me*. Sharing in their experience of great loss, I suddenly feel like I'm not alone. Here! Here is someone who has been burned to ashes in the same fire. Here is someone who has been lost in the same darkness. Someone who knows what lies past the line of the unthinkable. Someone who has traveled the same foreign landscapes as I and intimately knows every nuance of the long, winding, rocky path because they share the same bruising and scars that come from walking it. We share the same insights that can only be found by staring into the face of the terrible darkness, and now we know something deep in our bones that cannot be unknown. Our souls know each other now. And there is a real, genuine, authentic comfort in this, knowing we aren't alone.

Great loss gives us a new capacity. It burrows itself deep into our very soul, generating excruciating pain during the process, but after the heat of the dig subsides, a new tunnel is left behind. Strong as steel forged in fire or magma that has cooled for years, it leaves us with a new depth and capacity for understanding. Or perhaps appreciation is a better word. An appreciation for light, for beauty, for kindness, for peace, and especially for love. Or perhaps gift is an even better word. More on that later. Regardless of what we call it, this new capacity allows us the honor of meeting someone else lost in grief where they are. We cannot make the journey for them, but we can make sure they feel less alone. Again, there is a real, genuine, authentic comfort in having company on the long journey. It still hurts the same, but having company makes it all more manageable somehow.

So why am I writing about grief when it's been done before? Trust me, I struggled with that. But while I believe there are underlying human principles that unite us all, the ways we experience life, love, and loss are as unique as each one of us. If we defaulted to only one person's experience of grief, the first story would have been written, and we would all be content with those words. But no, there are thousands of grief stories out there. And each one is beautifully nuanced with the darks and lights and reflections and subtle shimmers and massive shifts that are unique to that person's expression. Just think about the millions of stories that are never written down. I find that humbling too.

All that being said, let me quickly add what this story is *not*. It's not an essay on religion or my beliefs. It's not a full narrative of my story with Mike when he was on this earth. It's not even a full account of the aftermath after his death. It's simply my best effort to articulate a small sliver of my story. Why? Well, maybe I can help someone *else* by giving *them* words to harness the slippery, intangible feelings that go along with grief, because doing so may offer some taming of the madness—even if it's just to let you know you aren't alone.

While I cringe a bit at the sound of my own footfalls gingerly tiptoeing on this sacred path, I am slightly emboldened to move forward by the fact that I have been given a gift. A rare and special gift indeed: the capacity for meeting others lost in grief and sharing their journey, for Lord knows I found comfort in the stories, words, and shared understandings of the grievers who have gone before me. So this is my attempt to share my story, as only I can tell it. Thank you for listening.

> We are all just walking each other home.
> —*Ram Dass*

1
THE BACKSTORY

We were together. I forget the rest.
—*Walt Whitman*

It was a storybook romance from day one, my personal fairytale come to life. We were young when we met. But what a catch Mike was! I remember falling so very, very deeply in love with him, and it all started from the day we met. I was only seventeen, and he was twenty-one. We met in karate class and started dating shortly thereafter, embarking on a sweet romance full of fire and starlight and all the exuberant and exciting things young love brings with it. Mike even went to my senior prom with me, and I was so proud to be with him. After all, he was *the* most handsome man I'd ever met or had even seen up to that point. I adored him. I was sure he should be a model or movie star. But unlike most of the cute boys I knew, he wasn't full of himself. Rather, he was quiet, humble, and kind. I found all those traits together to be an irresistible combination! As a young girl, I was completely head-over-heels infatuated with him. And well beyond his dashing looks and strong, silent demeanor, Mike had even more to offer. He had an inner light, positive energy, and pure authenticity that shined out to the world through his energy and smile. Everyone loved Mike. He was kind. He loved his family and friends, he loved animals, but best of all, he loved me too. Seeing the way he looked at me with those steely-blue eyes made me burn with fire inside. He brought out the very best in me, and with him by my side, I felt as though I could conquer the world.

He was a carpenter by trade and so very smart and competent at everything he tried. He was a master at solving problems. If a problem was given to him, he would quietly take it into his brain to absorb, process, and eventually solve—every time. There was never any drama or defeat, and usually there wasn't even any talking about it out loud. But I knew his mind was quietly sifting through solutions immediately, and by the next morning, he would have a plan. And it would always be a good one. He was good with his hands and incredibly creative. Naturally athletic and coordinated, he could conquer almost any sport with ease. What a catch he was! And I was constantly walking on clouds that he wanted to be with me. We were completely devoted to each other. We would talk and text daily. We had dates, planned surprises, and made each other laugh. It was a very happy time in my life.

We dated for five long, happy years before I finally graduated from college and we were free to be married. It was a beautiful wedding, if I do say so myself. Both of us cried during the ceremony, and I just couldn't have been happier or more in love with my new husband or our life together.

We leaned on each other during hard times and supported each other unconditionally. We traveled the world together. We had so many crazy adventures and had so much fun the entire time. It was never Mike and I against each other; it was always us as a team against the world. Always. Neither one of us was perfect, but we were perfect for each other. Our individual strengths and weaknesses complemented each other. Together, we were a force to be reckoned with! It made me brave.

Mike was my best friend. He always conspired to make all my dreams come true, and I did the same for him.

What we had was sacred. A deep friendship. A knowing. An understanding. Most of the time we didn't even need words.

We were married for sixteen years but together for twenty-one years. I was thirty-nine years old when the accident happened that took him away from us.

Yes, we were young when we met, and we had a lot of growing to do as individuals. I think that sometimes when people meet so early in life with all that developing left to do, they unfortunately grow apart. But the opposite happened to us. Instead, we grew together and our lives became intertwined. That union took on an identity of its own. We were two peas in a pod and known to almost everyone as "Mike and Dawn," almost as our collective title. I didn't know how much my identity was tied up in us until I lost it.

2
THE ACCIDENT

Love knows not its own depth until the hour of separation.
—*Kahlil Gibran*

It was June 21, 2016. A Tuesday.

The day started like an ordinary one. Well, it was wheat harvest—and nearing the end of the two-week event—so things were a little more hectic than usual.

Mike was up early that morning. Of course, he was usually up early every morning. It was his time. He loved to work out first thing each morning and mentally gather himself to prepare for the day. He had made his lunch and was getting ready to head out to the field. I could tell he already had a million to-do items parading through his mind.

I remember kissing him goodbye that morning. He was in the kitchen, preparing his lunch for the cooler. He was wearing his work clothes, which were nothing special, but they looked so good on him. He was dressed in a ball cap, cowboy boots, work jeans, and a simple T-shirt that was tucked in and accentuated his trim physique. He could have been conjured right out of a magazine. Thanks to his dedication over the past few years, he was currently in the best shape of his life, and knowing he had gotten up early to work out and prepare a healthy lunch, I couldn't help but smile at him in admiration. *You are so handsome,* I said in my mind. I should have said it out loud.

I could tell from his demeanor that he had a lot on his mind that morning. Wheat harvest was nearing an end, but there was still much to do before it was over—about a week left of cutting wheat and some pressure to get finished before the weekend. We had three separate social events competing for our attention that weekend. We wanted to celebrate our sixteenth wedding anniversary, my nephew Ben was getting married on Saturday, and Mike's friend Chris had an annual barbecue Mike wanted to attend in Wisconsin.

I knew he was struggling with how to *get it all done*, as harvest was bearing down on everyone at the same time. On that morning in particular, I knew he wanted to complete some maintenance tasks on the machinery while he still had a spell of quiet, before the hectic pace of the day took hold of him, colored with all the day's characters, personalities, and typical harvest drama. There was one moment in particular I won't forget, because it was my very last memory of him. I looked him in the eyes and casually kissed him goodbye like I did every morning, without any clue that would be the very last time I could do either. What I wouldn't give to get that moment back and savor it properly for what it was.

The day was a hectic one for me too. Work was so busy. Plus I had to take my sister to Salina for a doctor's appointment that morning, which was an hour's drive away. I was trying to jockey between returning phone calls to my important work clients, taking care of my sister, and trying to get home before lunch. I had my own doctor's appointment at 1:00 p.m. and wanted to make lunch for my niece Veronica before I left.

It was around 12:30 p.m. when I heard noise outside my front door. I recall I was on my phone, on hold with Blue Cross Blue Shield. I heard someone knocking on my front door. It was my dad. He knocked but didn't really wait for me to answer before he just barged in. I smiled at him as he stepped over the threshold, but he wasn't smiling. I could feel an urgent, chaotic energy enter the front door with him. And then I saw the priest, Father Damian, behind him.

My dad spoke, and I'll never forget what he said. "Dawn, there's been a tragedy."

I looked at him and could feel my pulse quicken. My mind struggled to catch up. A tragedy. Something bad had happened. Something terrible. I felt a sense of relief it wasn't my dad, and my mind instantly shifted to my mom. *Oh no. Mom.* Was she all right?

I felt an urge to call Mike immediately. I didn't know what terrible news was going to follow, but I knew I needed Mike to be with me. I barely knew what was wrong yet, but I needed to tell him about it. I needed him now.

My dad continued. "It's Mike. He was killed. It was an accident. It wasn't anyone's fault."

And so that's how, in an instant, the world as I knew and loved it ended forever.

And just like that, the thing most precious to me in all the world was gone.

There was a pinpoint of a moment of complete silence where time froze, suspended by impossibility. But then the words I heard became the thoughts that followed, and reality crashed in like a freight train.

My dad said, "Mike was working underneath the combine header. It came off the combine and fell down on him while he was working. He was killed instantly and did not suffer."

My dad. I look back on that moment now with such admiration of his strength and bravery. I realize now that he said three very important things I desperately needed to hear to prepare me to process the rest. He said the truth in as few words as possible. He let me know that there was no one to blame. And very kindly, he let me know that Mike didn't suffer.

> God made the world round so we would never be able to see too far down the road.
> —Isak Dinesen

The mind is a strange thing in how it reacts to the unthinkable. How it slips into denial, then shock, then pain.

Of course, I slipped immediately into that state of utter denial. I stared at my dad in disbelief. In that moment, someone could have more easily convinced my rational mind that aliens were outside my front door with a laser to blow up the world than the fact that Mike was gone.

This was not acceptable, to say the least. I *told* my dad it wasn't true. In fact, I couldn't say much else. Like an insane person, I repeated the words "It isn't true!" over and over and over. I stated them flatly. And then I screamed them at everyone in the room.

If pure resolve could have created something from nothing, I would have willed my desired reality into being. I grabbed the front of the priest's shirt with both my hands. I could see some alarm in his widened eyes at my gesture, and he leaned away from me, but

I didn't care if he was scared of me or thought I was crazy. I stared into his eyes and also proclaimed to him it wasn't true. He looked away.

That's when they all started praying. My dad, the priest, and more. They tried to surround me with protection by chanting prayers. I knew they had good intentions and might well have protected me with divine energy, but as for myself I utterly hated that moment. I didn't want any of that awfulness. I just wanted Mike.

My mom and sister both came through the front door, each with a look of desperation I'd never seen before. I looked at my mom and grabbed her hands, holding them in mine so dearly, and pleaded with her.

"It's not true."

I pleaded with my mom. I *begged* her. I remember her looking at me with a feeling of complete helplessness. Then when she couldn't bear it, she looked to my dad, her husband, in desperation, saying, "Donald, what are we going to do?"

She was as lost as I was. We were together then, my mom and I. We were both so very lost, and neither of us knew what to do.

I sank to my knees and dissolved in sobs on the floor. I couldn't stop saying, "It's not true," over and over. But I was whispering it now because I had no voice left in my lungs.

A police offer handed me Mike's wallet. I stared at it, resting there in my hands. It was a wallet he had gotten as a Christmas present. It was black leather bifold, well-worn and gently bowed from living in the back pocket of his jeans. It was the only physical connection I had with him in that moment. In a state of bleary-eyed despair, I opened the front flap. Halfway tucked inside the very front pocket was a beautiful medal of Saint Michael the Archangel. I stared at it in disbelief for a full twenty seconds, maybe more. Did Michael carry this item around with him all the time? I did not know that he did—and it seemed like an odd thing to find in the very front of his wallet for sure. I believe it was an important sign meant for me that Saint Michael was with him now, and a shiver went down my spine.

Within a period of twenty minutes, maybe less, my entire house was filled with dozens of people. Milling about through the entire house, even in the private areas like my office and master bedroom; normally I would have cared about the dust on the shelves or the laundry waiting to be folded, but thankfully all of that was beyond me. They all watched me have a complete mental and emotional breakdown in the middle of the room. It was probably like watching a train wreck. There was nothing anyone could do, and there was nowhere for me to go or hide from them or the reality that was crushing me now. I felt violated in almost every way, but mostly because something had taken away my most precious, sacred possession: my husband, my best friend, my marriage, my life, my future, my home. It was all gone.

3
THE AFTERMATH

It's your road, and yours alone. Others may walk it with you, but no one can walk it for you.

—*Rumi*

I sat on the floor in shock. Only a fraction of what had just happened had soaked into my mind, soul, and body, but it was enough to shake me to my core. I couldn't stop sobbing. My body transformed into a sob. The rest of me was empty, an empty space. The din of chaos, ill-formed thoughts, and the silent screams of despair and impossibility echoed loudly in my mind.

My brother walked over to me with a phone against one ear and gently tried to get my attention. I looked up at him with glassy eyes while he spoke to me in a quiet voice.

"Dawn, I'm on the phone with the funeral home. They would like to know what time you can meet with them tomorrow to pick out a casket and make funeral arrangements."

What kind of a question is that?

Well, I'll tell you it's a very practical one. Like, hey sure, let me check my schedule and get back to you! But I was not in a practical frame of mind, and just imagining the very notion felt as if someone had poured alcohol in a wound or stomped on a broken leg.

"How about one p.m.?" he said.

"Okay," I replied.

I glared at everyone else milling about in my house. People drifting like zombies through the living room, gathering in quiet corners to whisper about what had happened, and basically an entire audience of shocked bystanders watching me having a public meltdown. I knew they felt sorry for me, but I hated it. I hated the very notion that this unacceptable reality existed and that I was trapped in it like a cage.

The day progressed in agony, in spite of the impossibility of time going on. The clocks all still worked somehow. My spirit and soul were bruised, crushed, devastated, and that's only the tip of the iceberg.

My friend Father Keith called, and I remember being on the phone with him, just sobbing. He really didn't know what to say. I told him I could still feel Mike's presence, because I could. It was just that morning I had seen his face in person and kissed him goodbye as he walked out the door. That moment was only a breath away. I felt like the space in the kitchen where he stood that morning was still warm. I could almost hear his voice, feel his hand in mine, feel his arms wrapped around me in one of his bear hugs. It was all just a slip away.

Father Keith said he knew Mike was still with me, just not in the way I wanted him to be. So quickly these people were willing to accept the truth. How could they? Every inch of my consciousness was fighting to *not* accept it. I guess that's what's called the denial phase.

I don't remember much about that night; my body and mind ached, and the bed felt so cold and empty. I desperately wanted to feel the warmth of Mike's presence beside me, his arms wraxpped around me, and his fingers linked in mine. I reached for him over and over, but there was nothing in his space but the void he had left behind.

As the curtain of sleep threatened to cloak my consciousness, I was terrified of waking up and not remembering what had happened, only to live through the nightmare of remembering again. But I needn't have worried about forgetting. The harshness of the reality had seeped into every pore, like hot Jell-O into sponge cake, and every single cell of my body remembered. I don't even think I slept, at least not in the traditional sense. I think that perhaps my mind was so exhausted it collapsed into nothingness for a while, but that is a very different thing altogether.

The next morning we all went to the funeral home to pick out a casket from the many options they had on display. There were expensive caskets and inexpensive ones; fancy ones with scrolling and gold filigree and others that were wooden and plain.

All family members just gave me infinite space and supported all my decisions. I picked out a nice casket; certainly not the most expensive one, because I could all but hear Mike voicing his displeasure at such frivolousness. I could almost hear him say it was just going into the ground where no one would see it after the service.

Then we went back to my house to meet with the priest, Father Damian, and organize the funeral. I was beat down to a new low, literally just surviving. And there was still so much to do. I was torn between wanting to collapse and crawl under my bed and mustering the effort required to plan a beautiful tribute to Mike. So I suspended the gravity pulling me to give up on life, at least until after the funeral.

The task before us was daunting. We had to orchestrate a beautiful tribute to Mike's life and had less than twenty-four hours to do it, while I was fighting a total mental breakdown. But it was what he deserved. It was the last service I could offer him. I wanted to make sure he was honored appropriately. All of his family and friends would be there. Among the many tasks before us, we had to pick songs, Bible readings, participants, pallbearers, and more. Someone had to write an obituary, and I felt that someone needed to be me. We had to make a board display with photos of Mike. We had to decorate the casket with flowers and meaningful items. I was entirely overwhelmed, but I knew I could dig deep and get it done, because it was indeed something I was doing for Mike.

Unfortunately, my body had other ideas.

I couldn't eat, because eating food felt like trying to stuff Styrofoam into my mouth. But even without eating food, my blood sugar was very high. Since I am a Type 1 diabetic, stress can make my blood sugar increase. Blood sugar is one of the body's mechanisms to deal with a fight-or-flight situation; it floods the bloodstream with sugar (energy to the body) to deal with the acute stress.

But since my body lacks the ability to regulate an elevated blood sugar by making a corresponding amount of insulin, it doesn't take long for things to go a little haywire. The more acute stress involved, the more haywire things can go. I'd dealt with this issue of acute stress-related blood sugar spikes before, but I'd never in my life seen my blood sugar behave as crazy as this. It just couldn't be tamed. Before the family meeting with the priest to discuss the funeral, I had tested my blood sugar to see that it was high, at a level of 425 mg/dL (normal blood sugar range is 90–125 mg/dL). So ... 425 was not good.

I was nauseated, and my head was throbbing with a massive headache; both were symptoms of a high blood sugar for me. I took a large dose of insulin, maybe 10 units. Normally a dose of this amount would bring my blood sugar down within an hour or two. It certainly wouldn't increase it. But lo and behold, when I went to check it again after the meeting, it was well over 500. Not good.

I was fighting severe nausea now. I took *more* insulin, a lot more, and rejoined my family in the dining room. I felt sick and just wanted to be alone. I craved solitude and relief from all these voices and questions, and any outside stimuli for that matter, but I still had *so much* to do to prepare for the funeral.

My mind ran down my mental checklist. The funeral home still needed Mike's obituary written and submitted by ten the following morning, I still had to drop off Mike's hammer and tape measure at the florist so she could integrate them into the bouquet, and then we had a viewing of the body tomorrow morning too. I couldn't even wrap my brain around how horrible that last part was going to be. In a state of borderline panic, I stubbornly fought the weight of overwhelm that bore down on my psyche.

But as the afternoon wore on, I began to wear thin. I desperately wanted to be alone. And I so very much wanted to free myself of this mounting nausea and headache; those issues weren't convenient at *all*.

Eventually, the bulk of the funeral arrangements had been planned. One by one, family members and friends drifted out of the house. Finally only my dad was left behind. He stood in the hallway and looked at me with such gravity. He didn't say much; he just hugged me and asked me if I'd be okay. I told him yes. And then he left too, and I collapsed on the bed with a wave of nausea that would have knocked out an elephant. This was finally the respite I so desperately needed.

But just as my head hit the pillow, I knew I was in a bit more trouble. I felt my mouth start to salivate in preparation of vomiting. I had held it together till now, but now I could feel it all bubbling up. Violently. I ran to the bathroom and vomited fluids into the toilet. I instantly felt less nauseated and lay down in relief. The relief was short-lived. Within five minutes, I felt it happening again. I ran to the bathroom and lost more fluid laced with stomach acid that left my throat and mouth burning. I lay back down, for just a few minutes, before I had to do it all again.

And again. And again.

Okay, this wasn't going to work for me. I had *way* too much to do. But I also knew I really needed help. I needed to get to the hospital and get on an IV immediately. I'd had a similar experience with this sort of response from my body one time before, when I was in a serious vehicle rollover accident in Africa where my vehicle was swept into a river. While I wasn't physically injured in this accident in a serious way, I had so much emotional stress from the trauma that, for the next several hours, I couldn't keep my blood sugar down, and I couldn't stop vomiting. The doctor administered an IV of fluids and insulin to rehydrate me and get my blood sugar numbers down.

I remembered this incident well, so my body's response to this newest trauma was somewhat familiar. I already knew what needed to be done. I would just tell the doctors what to do, get it done, and then be on my way home to finish up the funeral planning tasks and writing the obituary. The obituary—that was already such a daunting task. How could I capture the value of Mike's entire life in a short essay? In case he was watching, I really wanted to make him proud. It gave me motivation and strength to persevere. But first, I had to get in and out of the hospital.

I called my sister-in-law, Jennifer. I stammered to her over the phone, "Jennifer, I need your help."

She replied bravely. "Yes, of course ... anything you need."

"Okay. I need a ride to the florist, to drop off these props for the casket bouquet. And then I need to go to the emergency room," I replied matter-of-factly.

There were a few moments of silence. "Emergency room?" she asked.

I did my best to explain. "I just need a quick IV. No big deal."

More silence. I could almost hear her silent questions. "I'll be right there," she finally said and hung up.

Within five minutes she had arrived, and we were on our way. Needless to say, we skipped the florist and went straight to the emergency room. I opened the car door and immediately vomited on the pavement outside the front door. I staggered through the entryway and was met by a nurse. She escorted me to an examination room, asked a few questions, and called in the doctor. While I was waiting for the doctor, I did my best to explain to the nurses that I didn't have a lot of time to waste. If they could just hook me up to an IV and get me some fluids and medicine, I could be on my way because I was very busy. They bobbed their heads to placate me until the doctor arrived. Upon examination, he proclaimed that I was going nowhere in the immediate future, but rather I needed to be admitted to the hospital immediately. I told him I really couldn't stay, but it was no use. I was very ill, and there was no denying it.

Jennifer dropped off the props to the florist and came back to be by my side. She stayed in the hospital room with me that entire awful night, sleeping in the uncomfortable chair next to me, if you can call it sleeping. My sister Ann stayed at my house and took care of my dogs. I told them both not to tell the rest of my family I was in the hospital because I didn't want Mom and Dad to worry. They had been through enough.

I agreed to the doctor that I would stay for the night on one condition, provided I could leave the next morning around nine a.m., before the showing of the body at the funeral home which was scheduled for ten. That's when the funeral home would display the body. I was so terrified of that moment, coming face to face with Mike's lifeless body, that I couldn't even think about it. I just knew I had to be there. Putting one thought in front of the other, but nothing more. The doctor simply said, "We'll see."

The nurses hooked me up to IVs on both sides of my body. I was connected to tubes and beepers and all sorts of equipment monitoring just about everything. The nurses in that unit smuggled in a laptop for me to type on, so that I could work on writing Mike's obituary. I wrote and cried and edited and sobbed and rewrote all night. Somewhere in the middle I was able to contact Mike's best friends, Andy and Chris, who lived in Wisconsin, to see if they could be pallbearers.

I was conflicted about asking them, because I wasn't sure if I should make them feel obligated to drive all that way at the last minute and jump through Lord knows what hoops with work or personal life to make it happen last minute, and I cringed a little knowing Mike would hate putting his friends out in any way, but something told me I needed to honor them by at least asking. Of course they both said they would come and agreed almost immediately. I wasn't surprised. These were good people and even better friends.

By dawn, I had the obituary written and had emailed it to the funeral home.

The bulk of the funeral was finally planned. What *wasn't* planned yet would get picked up by other people, but for the most part the heavy tasks were done.

With the IV of insulin, my blood sugar had stabilized through the night, the vomiting had ceased, and I was no longer in a state of severe dehydration. The doctor released me from the hospital, and I had just enough time to go home and change my clothes before people started dropping by the house.

We left for the ten o'clock appointment at the funeral home. The experience that followed was surreal and gut-wrenching. I approached Mike's open casket. He was lying there with his eyes closed, or should I say, I was really just gazing on the shell that was left behind, because Mike wasn't there. Seeing the likeness of his face was jarring to say the least, and to this day I cannot look at pictures of the open casket without feeling severe whiplash and nausea.

I know the funeral home did an amazing job with the appearance of his body and face, and I know that was a gift for many, including me. Even so, seeing Mike's body was a journey back to the scene of the accident that I wasn't even physically present for. Rather, I imagined it in my mind, what physically happened there. I told myself over and over that he didn't suffer. And those present for the accident agreed with me, that there was no way Mike knew what happened or suffered in any way.

I kneeled near the casket. My heart was broken. I felt crushed and completely defeated. I thought about all the *important* things that Mike had planned to do that day of the accident: the plans we were making to celebrate our anniversary; the last kiss goodbye on the cheek that I took so much for granted, so blissfully ignorant of the future.

My mind flashed to one of the last quiet moments we had before the accident. It was on June 17, our sixteenth wedding anniversary. My dad, brothers, and nephews were all working in the harvest field, at a field off Hyde Road, about three miles from our house. I had an anniversary card for Mike, and brought it out to the field that evening. It was the close of a long day for everyone in the harvest field, and the cool breeze of the evening paralleled the lightness of spirit that comes when a long, hard day is almost over.

Mike and some of the other guys were standing in the draw of the field, taking a pause while waiting for the combine to fill up the last load of wheat for the day. Banners of gold and pink washed across a muted blue sky in memory of the dying sun that had set moments before. Mike saw me pull up in my car to the field entrance, and he smiled at me with his eyes until the corners of his mouth followed. I can't help but smile now, just thinking about Mike's smile. We had a few moments alone together to bask in the quiet shelter of each other's company while the business of harvest and other people's accompanying chatter faded to trivial noise in the background, like a pause of respite in the storm. Mike always brought peace to my mind and soul.

THE FUNERAL

I can't write much on this—mainly because my mind is fuzzy on it, and the details are but a blur. I remember much beauty in the ceremony and the collective love surrounding me with all our family and friends. But overall, getting through that day was hell on earth.

4
THE NUCLEAR WINTER

And as the ashes of what was settled to the ground,
the dust of what should have been scattered in the wind.
The clocks stopped, the sky was grey and the birds were silent.
The world was suspended in the unearthly silence of complete surrender.
—*Athena Prost*

The following reflections describe the days immediately following the accident. It was the most difficult time of my life, and it changed me forever.

They say God doesn't give you anything you can't handle. I disagree. At least not without a dash of insanity.

CAN'T COMPUTE

The human brain is our interface with the world. It's an astonishing device! In many ways, I see it much like a computer—using hard data within its stash of resources to construct a model to process and define a given scenario. It uses data and programs, the best it can, to make sense of what's happening to us and around us. It optimizes and problem-solves on our behalf.

So it's utterly astonishing how the brain tries to compensate when faced with an impossible scenario that it literally cannot compute. It's a special type of insanity. A computer stuck in a loop, shorting out, solving for an unsolvable riddle, lost in a broken code.

My own brain, bless it, did the most startling things to try and help me make sense of this impossible scenario in front of me. Mike is gone. Forever? *Nope*. How could that be? It's *impossible*. It's *unacceptable*. There is no working program for this.

But still, here we were, neck deep in the middle of the impossible, and my brain had to do something. So it spoke to me—visually. I suppose a mere vocabulary of words didn't contain enough depth to harness the emotions I was feeling, let alone give my brain the raw materials it needed to process the pain and the loss, so it made movies instead.

THE VISIONS

I've never had visions before in my life. But that changed after I lost Mike, as my brain struggled to frame my new reality in a way that my mind could actually process. My poor, unequipped mind had never seen or felt anything like this before, and it flailed about in a panic, using scraps from my life experiences and my imagination to construct tangible models of my grief in my mind's eye that I could grasp. And thus came the visions.

My first visions were of a monster—a terrible, hulking, giant monster that raised its ugly head and towered over me, several stories high. It could easily crush me at will. It had thick and massive horns like a bull and a huge dragon-like mouth full of fangs that glistened in a strange, otherworldly light. It had reptilian skin and scales, and it breathed fire. Its eyes glowed yellow and fierce and had no pupils. But the most impressive feature of this monster was its sheer size and dominating presence. It was hundreds of feet high, and in spite of my tiny and insignificant size, its gaze was focused fiercely on me. I was tiny and insignificant in its shadow, and I felt it. I had no choice but to cower and collapse on the floor to my knees in a helpless, hopeless surrender, to surely be crushed. I was totally and completely defeated.

My second vision was of a void. I was standing on the precipice of a cliff, and beside me was a bottomless pit of darkness; a gaping chasm in the earth, black and empty. I could sense it was endless and devoid of life and hope. It sucked in all the light around it, all the air and hopes and dreams and beauty. It smelled of death and loss and loneliness and panic. The abyss was directly behind me. I would tentatively peek over my shoulder from time to time, to catch a tragic glimpse of it, but then I would look away because it was too much to bear.

Directly in front of me was the rest of the world. People going on with their daily lives, shopping, working, talking, and laughing, completely and alarmingly oblivious to this gaping void right behind me that was sucking in the oxygen all around me. It threatened to pull me right into its belly to be consumed and forgotten.

How could the other people around me not see it? How could they not stare and scream and run? I wanted to tell them and to show them, but they would never believe me or understand it. Again and again, I peered over my shoulder to check, and sure enough the dark chasm was still right there, directly behind me, looming and sucking and black and threatening. I was so dangerously close to the edge that a mere breeze would be enough to make me lose balance and fall into its yawning, infinite darkness.

The presence of the void was undeniable to me, and the gravity of it was overwhelming. I was constantly fighting a full-blown panic attack that was simmering right under the surface. But somehow I stayed standing, even keeping my composure, with my back to the abyss. I faced the people in front of me and never said a word about the void. Somehow I was able to pretend my entire world wasn't disappearing into it as life went on as always for everyone else.

My third vision was of myself trapped in a small, enclosed room without a door. I was facing four blank, featureless walls. There had to be a way out, right? I paced. I had to get out. Then I panicked. I ran in endless circles around and around the doorless room, desperately seeking a door, a solution, a way out to the life I had. I was like a caged animal that was fighting for its life, frantically looking for a door, a solution, a way out. There was none. I was trapped. Eventually I collapsed on the floor in utter exhaustion. I wouldn't have even known that level of emotional and physical exhaustion was possible if I hadn't directly experienced it.

THE PAIN

Alarmingly, in the immediate aftermath of the accident and for several weeks after, my body was in a constant state of physical pain, even though I had no evidence of being physically injured in any way.

Of course I was in shock and severe mental agony, all understandable after a sudden, tragic accident. But bizarrely enough, this all manifested itself into various forms of physical pain. I can't explain how, but I know the physical pain was very, very real.

So in great detail, my mind made mental movies of what was happening to me. A hammer. Road rash. A hot stove. And more. I imagine this was my brain at work again, trying to invent some scenario from its attainable frame of reference that would explain a source for such incredible physical pain.

First of all, and this happened twenty times a minute in the beginning, I would feel a violent jolt to my head, as if I'd just been hit by a hammer. As if some nameless, faceless person came and literally brought a real hammer down right on the top of my head. It happened every time I thought about the accident—every time I thought about my dad coming in the door to tell me the news or about Mike under the combine, or some other demented thought that would come charging rudely through my brain without my permission, and I would feel an intense jarring that could only be described as a violent, abrupt, intense physical pain. And while the frequency of this feeling slowly diminished over time, from twenty times a minute to fifty times a day to twenty or fifteen or ten times a day and so on. This went on and on for days, weeks, and even months.

Secondly, my body ached, and my skin burned. I would lie in bed or sit in a chair or on the floor, and it felt just as though I had a terrible case of road rash over my entire being. My body and mind both seared and throbbed in agony. I would close my eyes and see a mind movie of myself being dragged down an asphalt road behind a car, until my skin had been shredded off my body.

So what was really happening to me? Not being a psychologist, I can only speculate, but I can recall having a very mild experience with road rash years earlier when I was a child. One time at recess outside the grade school, I had fallen and skinned my knee on a concrete sidewalk. I speculate my brain found that scrap of experience in my memory archives and pulled it forward to assign the pain I was feeling to something rational. Road rash was the most accurate description of how I felt for a long time.

Thirdly—and this happened only at specific times when I saw a picture of Mike—my mind reacted by putting me into a story where I was reeling back after touching a hot stove and burning my hand, and again my mind roared with pain.

Finally, I just felt myself in a constant state of nausea and headache. My insides ached. My stomach was tied up and twisted. My head hurt and throbbed. And my mind was rocked in sobbing fits even after my physical eyes ran out of tears.

GOD

For days after Mike's accident my mind was just screaming at me. I survived those first few days, but I'm not sure how, and it was all terrible agony. There was no peace or sleep, only pain—mental, physical and spiritual pain.

I was so angry at God. I felt I had trusted Him, and in return He had dropped me on the floor. We were not speaking. In fact, it barely occurred to me to even consider talking to Him.

But I'll never forget the *exact* moment I finally asked God for help. I was sitting at the dining room table, with my head down on the table, and I had officially reached my breaking point. I picked up some rosary beads that had been sitting on the table nearby. The amber and blue crystal beads glinted in the afternoon sunlight that spilled in through the dining room window, and it caught my attention. It was a rosary that I had purchased from a street vendor when I was on vacation with Mike in Spain several years prior. I held them tightly.

I'm not sure where I got the energy to try it, but somehow I sobbed my way through a fifteen-minute rosary. Sometime during the course of this rosary, and for the very first time since the accident, it finally occurred to me to ask God for help. No, I begged Him.

And suddenly, right on cue, I felt this overwhelming sense of peace and relief just wash over me. The feeling was immediate, intense, all-encompassing, and downright tangible. Like a cooling salve or balm on a burn, it was pain-numbing, yes, but felt much more satisfying than that. I felt light.

I stopped crying for the first time in days. I sat up, put leashes on my three dogs, and went for a walk outside. The breeze was cool and colored with sweet summer scents, and puffs of white clouds floated above us. The dogs and I walked all the way to the cemetery and sat in the grass next to Mike's grave, and the peace just intensified. I closed my eyes and let myself dissolve in the sunlight and become absorbed by the immense blue sky.

Later that night, I fell asleep the moment my head hit the pillow and slept the entire night through. And it's been that way ever since.

The experience was so special and magical, and still is, that there is no doubt in my mind that this peace was a divine gift. And then it occurred to me, for the very first time: I may never understand the reasons for the events that unfold in life. But regardless, maybe God is on my side after all. Maybe, just maybe, I should let Him.

AFRICA

One especially interesting thing happened when I went to Africa. To give this experience some context, my primary day job is in the travel industry, helping people plan safari trips to East Africa. I've done it for years, and I love Africa at a deep soul level. A grand side benefit of my job is that I get to go to Africa on work assignments from time to time. In fact, I often got to share the experience with my husband, Mike, and I have many memories of our shared times there together.

In August of that year, just two short months after the accident, my boss Michael asked if he could send me on safari in Africa. I think he sincerely wanted to help me but didn't know how, and this was something he could do. Africa, and the beauty of the wide expanses of nature there, can be a source of inner peace for many and a potent tonic for weary hearts, so perhaps it was worth a try.

But going to Africa is a *big* trip! Planning for any trip away from home, in my state, still required what felt like an insurmountable amount of mental and emotional energy. And if I'm being honest, I really didn't want to go. I didn't even want to get out of bed, brush my hair, or eat. How could I get on a plane and travel for twenty-five hours, fighting airport lines, security, and jet lag? Just the thought wore me out. But in spite of it all, I agreed to go. After all, Michael was just trying to do something nice for me, and even more honestly, I just felt too weak to say no.

One major upside to going this time was that I had the opportunity to bring my brother Brent with me. He had never been to Africa before, and I had always wanted to share it with him. So it was decided. Brent and I would make the journey to Africa, and we would be on safari for roughly two weeks.

My posse of amazing family and friends rallied around me to make it happen. Together we delegated who would take care of my horses, my dogs, my house, and my work. All I had to do was focus on preparing for the trip. Perhaps that sounds easy enough, but in spite of the fact I had been to Africa fifteen times before, going on an international trip of that level still requires a lot of effort. It's no small task to coordinate flights, organize travel documentation, and pack appropriately, along with assisting a new person who has never been on safari before to successfully do the same. If it hadn't been for the fact my brother was going to get to enjoy this trip too, I don't think I could have mustered the extra energy it took to get ready for such a big trip. I dug deep.

By departure time, my wits were frayed and my soul ached. To my dismay, I was experiencing a new anxiety, what I can only assume was a form of post-traumatic stress disorder. The logic-centered part of my brain was trying its best to calm my nerves, but I was still absolutely convinced something terrible was going to happen to my family while I was away. I needed to be near them, to try and protect them. I really felt as if someone else was going to die in another tragic accident or illness. I almost canceled the trip, but there was too much momentum behind it now, and I didn't have the energy to stop it. I was in survival mode, and it was all I could do to go with the flow.

Inevitably, the departure day eventually arrived, and it was time to go. I said goodbye to my sister Ann and my friends Brenna and Shae, who were all taking turns watching my house and taking care of my beloved dogs while I was away.

I remember drifting through the motions of travel, ghosting through airports and plane rides, with my brother at my side, who was smart enough to give me a much-needed margin of silence for most of our journey. We arrived in Africa, and as the plane touched down, I was instantly flooded with a thousand bittersweet memories, since Mike and I had shared so many exclusive adventures in this remote place. Africa was ours.

I spent most of the next several days in the very back of the jeep. My brother was in the jeep as well, but he sat closer to the front of the vehicle, and for the most part he just let me be. During those hours of solitude, I let Africa wash over me. I let myself get lost in the rhythm of the bumping and jostling as the vehicle lumbered over the rocky, rutted roads. I listened to the birds and felt the sun on my face and breathed in a thousand smells that saturated the tropical air. I let the dust swirl around me, and I lost all track of time except for the placement of the sun in the sky. I felt myself dissolve into the surrounding nature—the rumble of a thousand stampeding wildebeest, the cries of the lonely fish eagles above, and the endless blue of the sky. The solitude of this infinite nature was probably the very best medicine I could have taken.

But then the night would come. I shared a room with my brother Brent. We had separate beds, but it was comforting to know he was there in the room with me. Night was a very difficult time for me. As darkness descended, so did my fears. The harshness of my new reality, along with paralyzing fears of something terrible happening to my family back home, would close in around me. Africa can feel intimidating at times; it's so big, remote, and exotic, and while nature can be beautiful, it can also be quite harsh. The circle of life claims its victims here freely, and there is nothing to buffer the inherent cruelty that is woven into the very design of life. The feeling of vulnerability that comes from being at the mercy of something bigger and unknown was all amplified at night, as the black sea of darkness surrounded me.

One night, something strange happened to me. In the middle of the night, while I was sleeping soundly, a loud, booming voice jarred me awake. The voice was as real as if it came from a person sitting right next to me, and the space around me seemed to continue to reverberate with its intensity. At an alarmingly loud volume, it had pronounced the words, "Your dad is *dead.*"

I lay completely still in my bed, frozen in terror and afraid to move, with my eyes wide open, desperately searching through the fuzzy darkness around me for some clue as to who was speaking. The voice sounded demonic to me.

I looked over to my brother's side of the room. It seemed impossible, but he was still sleeping peacefully, as indicated by the cadenced rise and fall of his heavy sleep breathing. I couldn't understand it. How could he possibly sleep through that voice?

I lay in bed wide awake for the rest of the night, until I could finally see the gradual light of dawn gently illuminating the space outside. I never did hear the voice again.

I can never say for sure what happened that night, but I feel *something* had come to prey on my vulnerable mind, my fear, and my broken heart. I couldn't wait to call my dad that morning! I scrambled to find a phone to call him, and I sighed in relief at the sound of his voice. I'm happy to say, he was not dead!

5
REFLECTIONS ON GRIEF

Below are a series of reflections on grief, in no particular order, that I wrote while I was going through my evolution. Some are from deep in the tunnel, but I share them here because they are a part of my story. And maybe I'll meet someone where they are in their journey to remind them they aren't alone.

THE THINGS PEOPLE SAY

First of all, I don't think there is anything *good* to say to a grieving person at a time like this. I think the best advice I could give a friend or family member of a grieving person is to say minimal words, but just show up for them. There is really nothing you can do or say that will help solve the grieving person's real problem, in that the person they loved and cherished is gone and there is no bringing that person back. So you can't solve an unsolvable problem. But for the grieving person, there can be real comfort in your presence, in your love, and in simply knowing they aren't alone.

Some of the seemingly benign and well-intended things people said to me were still very hurtful. But I gave every single person the grace of a free pass, because I know. I know everyone struggles with what to say in the wake of profound loss, so I just shifted my focus from their words to their intent. Even if they were ignorant or broken or clumsy with their words, they were trying in the best way they knew how. It was beautiful they were showing up for me at all when the easier thing to do is to walk away or hide. I appreciated each one.

That being said, here were some of the hardest sentiments to process.

"How are you?"

This seems like an innocent, benign question. And on the surface it is. But a grieving person doesn't know how to answer it. Every time I heard this question, an inner conflict would arise in my mind and heart. I knew the person asking the question wanted to hear that I'm fine. Of course, the truth is that I'm *not* fine. I'm the furthest thing from fine! And to say or even imply I'm fine feels like a betrayal to the person who has passed. But I also know the person asking doesn't want to deal with the raw truth, and really, if I'm being honest, there is nothing that person could do with an answer beyond "I'm fine" anyway. So I jumped to saving us all the hassle and the awkwardness and released them all with the lie, "Yeah, I'm fine." That was what I did most of the time.

"Everything happens for a reason" or *"It's all part of God's plan."*

Okay. First of all, how the hell do *you* know? Are you privy to some supernatural knowledge about how the universe works and the secret content of God's day planner? To make a declaration like that makes you seem like an arrogant, pretentious know-it-all. Personally, I don't think this was part of God's plan at all. And my brain can't process a God who could intentionally *plan* for something so horrific. Did you ever consider the fact that perhaps God didn't plan for this at all, but sometimes bad things happen anyway? In the short term, and without yet possessing a greater knowledge of the infinite unknown, I have to assume

God is on my side, not planning things that will hurt me or those I love.

Again, the best gift of all is your presence. These are the people who helped me the most: the ones who just showed up for me, sat with me and cried with me, and held that space for me. Consequently, I think the most beautiful thing you can do for a grieving person is just show up with a sincere heart and say very little or nothing at all. The space will fill with the love and humility of a sincere heart, and the silence pays tribute to the magnitude of what words cannot express.

FIRE AND ASH

One unexpected side effect of my loss is that I desperately wanted to burn everything in a fire. I fantasized about a *huge* fire—hot flames glowing red and orange. I wanted it to consume all of my material possessions: my clothing, my shoes, knickknacks off my shelves, furniture, jewelry, pictures, every book on the shelf, and souvenirs I'd gathered from around the world. Even my house. The giant fire would engulf all my worldly possessions. The material stuff I used to admire and collect; the fire would turn it all to gleaming embers, black smoke and gray ash. And maybe I would find some justice in the sacrifice. As if someone had suddenly pulled back a cover that had previously cloaked my eyes, I could now see it all so clearly. That's all the value those material things had anyway. They were nothing more than a temporary incarnation of ash. It was all just ashes underneath. And I wanted to make it so.

This desire to burn down my house, including all my material possessions, was not a thought I shared with other people. Perhaps I was slightly insane, but I was still cognizant enough to know that those types of thoughts might not be accepted by the rest of society in a positive light. People might think I was crazy, or worse; they might worry these thoughts would result in my doing physical harm to my surroundings or myself. The thoughts didn't go away, but I held on to them in silence.

One day, several months after the accident, I finally confided these rather disturbing thoughts to one person. Lesley had lost her own husband to cancer a few years before Mike's accident, so she had already walked a path of trauma and grief before me, and I felt she understood me at a unique level. One day, as we were sharing thoughts and stories of our grief, the words just slipped out. I told her I had really wanted to burn everything in a fire. I immediately reeled back at the insanity of what I had just said and looked down at my feet, wishing I could take it back.

To my surprise and relief, she just looked at me calmly, smiled and said, "Me too! Only I actually did it!" She giggled a little.

Then she calmly proceeded to tell me how she started a large bonfire and burned up many of their household possessions, right after her husband John died—pictures off the wall, items she had collected, books, large pieces of furniture, and more. Wow! Her story was terrible, but at the same time I felt validated in this common thread that united us, and it was such a relief to know I wasn't as crazy as I thought. Or at the very least, I wasn't alone!

LONELINESS

I wasn't prepared for the loneliness. And it wasn't about being around other people; no, I had plenty of opportunity for that. I could be with a dozen members of my family and friends, but still feel completely and utterly alone. It was a loneliness so deep and powerful I almost couldn't handle it. Getting through each moment of each and every day was like trying to wade through a sea of thick Jell-O. I was moving through the day, yes, but each step forward felt heavy and exhausting.

My soul desperately searched for Mike. I ached for his physical presence. I would have given anything to see that sparkle in his blue eyes, followed by an upward curve on the corner of his mouth, signaling the beginning of a private smile reserved for me. With a glance across a room, we could share a dozen thoughts with each other without saying a word. I longed for my hand to fall into the warmth of his, our fingers so effortlessly finding their place interlaced with the other's. I yearned to hear his quiet chuckle or bask in the light of his smile. When Mike smiled, it wasn't just with his mouth. He smiled at you with his eyes, energy, and soul.

MEMORIES

Mike. I try to remember the sound of your laugh. I can almost hear it. But I can't quite.

I try to remember how my fingers linked up with yours when we held hands. How my hand fell so effortlessly into yours as we walked side by side. We always held hands, didn't we? Just walking from the car to the church door, or to a restaurant. It was something we always did, like breathing. Now, I can't remember how it went. Was my hand under or over yours? My thumb—where did it go? My eyes well up with tears at the impossible tragedy of forgetting, until I dissolve into a full-blown sob.

I run my fingers over your favorite sweatshirt. It's not quite you, but enough of you that it feels sacred. It's as close as I can get.

I look at the pages I have left of your handwriting. Pencil marks on lined paper. Your workout notes, a small artifact left behind to document a fraction of all the huge effort, sweat, and tears you put into those early morning workouts before the sun was up, on hundreds of mornings. And your construction notes scribbled on engineering graph paper, numbers and calculations, ghosts of all the brilliant thinking and problem solving and talent and creativity that pulsed with life in that beautiful mind of yours. These pencil marks are almost all the evidence I have left that those thoughts happened at all. Well, that and all the beautiful things you built with them. Many of those items are left behind. I run my hands over the cherrywood cabinets you constructed with love, and I think about all the beautiful things that will never be built now. Beautiful, intricate, original ideas that lived in your brain that I'll never know now. They all died with you.

Sometimes when I look at the night sky and gaze at the stars above, I think about their light and how real it is, for me, in my present moment. The reality is, that star died thousands if not millions of years ago. It no longer exists in our physical world, yet I am somehow presently bathed in its light, very real for me in that moment. Such are the memories of you for me. The warmth of your touch, the sound of your laugh, the light in your eyes and smile. Like yesterday. Like today. As if I could reach through the folds of time and feel your presence again. You are gone, but you are also still here with me.

Mike was more than just a partner to me. He was a feeling. He was warmth. He was light. He was peace. He was home.

HOMESICK

> And then she knew, that you could become homesick for people too.
> —*Beau Taplin*

The first few weeks after Michael left this world dissolved into a whirlwind of emotions. The shock had finally subsided, or at least it had evolved. But the heartache I felt now was almost unbearable.

Homesick is the only word that comes to mind. Reminiscent of that same homesick feeling I had when I was a little kid at summer camp, away from home for the first time. Only times a million.

Michael was home to me. We could be traveling in some exotic place, several thousand miles away from our house in Kansas, but when my hand would fall into his, I was home. When our gaze would connect across a room, I was home. When he would flash me a smile, or when I would hear his voice and laugh, even if it was just over the phone, I was instantly home.

It's very, very hard to accept the fact that I can never go home again.

RIDICULOUS

It all seems so ridiculous to me. All of us walking around and pretending life is normal, as if the world hadn't just ended. Because it did. But we still get up in the morning, go to work, come home, watch TV, go to bed, etc. My brain and every cell of my being rejects the audacity that life is supposed to continue.

Every time I find myself acting *normal*—simply going about my daily activities, making coffee, sweeping the floor, getting groceries, whatever—I feel like a fraud! What a façade. Because how can I go along with life as normal when nothing is normal? Nothing is okay. The world ended, remember?

It's the very definition of insanity to me.

PANIC

One of the most alarming and unexpected emotions I struggled with was feeling as if I was on the verge of a complete panic attack. I felt trapped. Trapped in this new life I didn't choose, dealing with circumstances I didn't ask for. My entire life plan, over twenty years in the making, had been suddenly cancelled, and a new life had been laid before me. I didn't want any part of it.

DEVASTATION

It was as if the rest of my life had been a happy movie. It almost felt like a dream. But now, this was my new, cold reality. This was real in a way I had never experienced reality before. It was so big, horrible, and crushing. It took all the oxygen out of the air so I couldn't breathe. It took all the strength from my legs and arms. My mind screamed in a language I'd never heard before, of deafening agony. I felt trapped in the chaos of a war zone in my mind, with explosives detonating all around me. I couldn't hear my own thoughts. My heart ached. My soul felt raw and ripped in two. The weight of it all brought me to my knees with my head in my hands and a complete loss of will to live. I was completely and utterly devastated.

GRIEVING TWO THINGS

As the days between me and the accident unfolded, some things became more apparent. What was previously just a huge glob of "overwhelm" started to get some space and definition. It flattened out a bit, and little nuances that weren't previously visible to my paralyzed mind finally started to come to light. I won't call it clarity, because that still isn't a word that fits this situation. I did not yet have clarity. But still, the grief had started to evolve, and my mind started to generate ideas, concepts, and words to better capture the abstract emotions I'd been swimming in.

As I continued to struggle to come to terms with what had happened, I started to realize the complexity of grief. I could see there were two grief tracks to follow, because I'd had to deal with two deaths, not one.

First of all, I had to grieve the *death* of *Mike*—the beautiful individual who lost his life far too young, too soon, and too tragically. Years later, this is still a subject I can't talk about without the sting of tears rushing to my eyes. It's so difficult to accept the death of someone so young, healthy, hardworking, fit, happy, caring—so full of promise, kindness, talent, potential, and love. He deserved better. He deserved the *best*.

The sheer injustice of it all is infuriating. The pain of the loss is crushing.

Mike lost his *life*, the ultimate loss, and that fact alone brings me to my knees, because I wanted nothing but the best for him. His family lost a husband, son, brother, uncle, nephew, grandson, and friend that day. This world in general is a dimmer, darker place because we lost his shining light. So there is *that* to grieve, and I share this grief with all our family and friends. I will never, ever get over this loss and this pain, as long as I live.

But for me it doesn't stop there. When Mike died, not only did I grieve the death of the individual and the role he played in my life, the husband and the best friend, but I also had to grieve the death of *us*. Because not only did I love Mike with all my heart, but I also loved *us*! The concept of *us* had taken on its own identity, which also died that day. Wow, did I love us. Not only were Mike and I a husband and wife, we were such a great *team*. When Mike died, I lost my life too, in a way. I lost the beautiful life I knew and loved. I lost the life we had worked almost our entire lives for. The life and future we had both cultivated so carefully and deliberately over twenty years of being together, and miles of future lay in front of us. Suddenly, that entire life track was derailed in spectacular fashion—along with all those mutual investments of time and energy of our past, and all our hopes and dreams for the future. They had crashed and burned and now were gone.

I lost my center. I lost my purpose. I lost my present and my future. I still have beautiful memories of our past, but they are bittersweet because they are mine alone now. I lost the hopes for all the smiles and laughter that would have someday been ours to share, as we sat on the sofa in our old age flipping through all the photographs and journals so carefully kept and documented, reminiscing about our adventures. The day Mike died, *us* died too. Mike lost his life, *and I lost the person I was, when I was with him.*

I didn't really like my life anymore.

It was like going from color to black-and-white.

And *that* is the challenge in front of me now: how to carry on with a new track, how to rebuild, how to create a new life and a new future. This is all quite daunting under the best of circumstances, but I have to say it's especially hard when you were so in love with your old life that you don't even want to try.

The death of a spouse or partner is different than other losses, in the sense that it literally changes every single thing in your world going forward. When your spouse dies, the way you eat changes. The way you watch TV changes. Your friend circle changes (or disappears entirely). Your family dynamic/life changes (or disappears entirely). Your financial status changes. Your job situation changes. It affects your self-worth. Your self-esteem. Your confidence. Your rhythms. The way you breathe. Your mentality. Your brain function. (Ever heard the term "widow brain"? If you don't know what that is, count yourself as very lucky.) Your physical body. Your hobbies and interests. Your sense of security. Your sense of humor. Your sense of womanhood or manhood. EVERY. SINGLE. THING. CHANGES. You are handed a new life that you never asked for and that you don't particularly want. It is the hardest, most gut-wrenching, horrific, life-altering of things to live with.

—*Kelley Lynn*

SOLE KEEPER OF THE MEMORIES

I had pictured Mike and myself growing old together—looking back over scrapbooks chock-full of pictures, movie stubs, and plane tickets, remembering all the happy, sad, stressful, and joyful times we shared together as a couple. But now I'm the only one left. I'm the sole keeper of the memories now.

The fact that these precious memories meant something to Mike is what gave them true meaning to me... because I *loved* him and because we *shared* it. Now he was gone, and I was left alone holding our bag of gold.

> Love is stronger than death, even though it can't stop death from happening, but no matter how hard death tries, it can't separate people

from love. It can't take away our memories either. In the end, life is stronger than death.

—Anonymous

PHOTOGRAPHS

It was a long time before I could even look at a photograph of Mike without experiencing a searing pain. The pain was intense in the initial days, weeks, and months after the accident—not unlike holding my hand on a hot stove or hitting my head hard on a metal beam.

Over time, this pain was cloaked in thin layers of new days and throbbed itself into a chronic ache, but it was always simmering just under the surface as real life marched on in its cold and cruel cadence. One careless thought, one glace in an old cardboard box of belongings, one look into a photo album, one poignant comment from a family member or friend, one brush up against one of Mike's old sweatshirts in the back of the closet, and the pain was renewed. The giant would rear its ugly head far above me and roar ... a presence so big and terrible I would cower beneath it, hitting my knees and dissolving back into uncontrollable sobbing.

I look at a photograph of myself before the accident, and I don't feel like that same person any longer. It's almost like I'm looking at a stranger.

THE FALLOUT

No one tells you what to expect when the dust has settled.

One thing I certainly didn't expect was that my hair would fall out. Not all of it, and not immediately, mind you. But I lost about half of it. It started to fall out about two months after the accident. I would be standing in the shower, letting the hot water pour over my body, and reach up to shampoo my hair. As my fingers combed through my long tresses, instead of sliding through the strands of hair as I expected, my fingers came away coated in hair. I would pull out clumps of hair at a time. It would cover the shower floor. To say it was alarming would be an understatement. And then I would sob and sob.

I can only speculate that this physical reaction of losing my hair was a result of the shock of the day of the accident that did it. My system underwent such an incredible shock that my hair literally fell out.

I did my best to hide it with ponytails and hats. The only person I told at first was my hairdresser, Cathy. Cathy was a kindred spirit anyway, who also loved Mike. I would sit in her chair to get my hair done, and we would both sob together. One day, several months after the accident, with giddy excitement she told me she could see my hair growing back! A little more fuzz appearing on my scalp, she said. And we laughed. It was a small sign of hope that maybe better days were ahead.

THE DREAMS

Nothing in life had prepared me for the dreams I was about to experience. It was as though my logical mind was grappling with this new problem and trying to find ways to reconcile the unthinkable new fact that Mike was gone. One way it did this was dreams—mostly nightmares.

I would dream about Mike at night. Most of the dreams wove some far-fetched story about Mike leaving me. Hardly any of them were comforting. They were all very different from each other, but none of them made much sense. The one common denominator in each of them was that at the end of each mini-movie, Mike was gone. And I also felt an overwhelming sense of loss and panic at the end of each one.

These nightmares were thin, foggy, low-quality dreams, peppered with *some* real memories, like watching old home movies on the projector that had been damaged or had sat in the attic too long.

In one story, Mike was driving the two of us in his truck. It was a warm summer day, and the windows were down. We were talking and enjoying each other's company. He parked on the grass next to the St. John's football field. I opened my passenger side door, stepped outside the truck and shut the door behind me. I bent down to tie my shoe. When I stood back up and peered through my window over to the driver's side door again, getting ready to say something to Mike, I noticed he was gone. Just like that, he had disappeared.

In another story, Mike and I had gotten into a big fight. (In real life we never fought.) In this dream, he was really angry. We were standing opposed to each other, at the end of a dim, empty hallway it what seemed like a high school. Mike turned away from me in anger, threw up his hands in frustration, and walked away. I felt helpless and sad as I watched him walk down the hallway, and finally out through the double doors at the end into the bright sunlight outside. For some reason I waited till he was out of sight, then I finally got my wits about me and ran after him to apologize and make amends.

By the time I stepped outside the doors, there was no trace of Mike except for his wallet, sitting on a ledge just outside the door. Instantly I knew something was very wrong, and he must be in trouble to be leaving his wallet behind, and I needed to find him. I found some friends and we got in a vehicle and drove up and down every street in Beloit, desperately searching for some trace of Mike, but he was nowhere to be found.

Those were two examples, but there were probably a half dozen variations of this abandonment dream. I would wake up each morning feeling even more alone, helpless and dejected.

Finally, after waking up in tears after yet another nightmare, I knew I had reached my breaking point. I cried and prayed in desperation, asking for help from Mike or God or anyone who was listening.

That very same night, I had another dream. But this one was different. This dream was much more powerful and vivid than the others, like a high-definition movie compared to the broken-down projector. In this new, high-def dream, I was walking down a country road in the springtime. The sun was out and grass grew green on both sides of the road. The ground was wet from a recent rainfall, and the air smelled cleansed and fresh. There was no sound except for the crunching of the gravel under my sneakers. My dear friend Cathy was walking by my side. We walked down that road together for a long time, neither of us saying anything, until finally we found ourselves at a bend in the road. I could see a building up ahead—a large structure of dark, weathered wood that resembled an old barn.

Cathy and I walked right up to the building and stepped through the front doors into a large room. I could see Mike was at the far end of the room, standing next to Cathy's husband, Matt. They were grilling burgers and hot dogs! At the sound of our arrival, they both turned around and looked at us. Mike made direct eye contact with me, and then he smiled. It was a big smile. It was all Mike. I remember how blue his eyes were—ice blue, but gentle—and he seemed to be made up of both matter and light. I was so happy to see his familiar face! I walked up to him, and he immediately wrapped his arms around me in the most beautiful, warm bear hug I'd ever experienced. I buried my face in his chest and dissolved into the peace of the moment. Without either of us saying anything, I felt a deep knowing from him that he loved me more than ever, that he would *never* leave me, and in the end everything was going to be all right.

This last dream was a beautiful moment, and I'll never forget it. Even though I still had a long road of grief evolution ahead of me.

COPING

So how do you survive the unsurvivable? Indeed, it's tricky.

MY FAMILY AND FRIENDS

> You are the finest, loveliest, tenderest, and most beautiful person I have ever known—and even that is an understatement.
>
> —*F. Scott Fitzgerald*

My family and friends were too brilliant to even give due credit here. What beautiful souls they all were. Whether it was helping with the funeral or taking care of my dogs and horses, bringing me food or going to the store, absorbing my daily errands or taking care of my work tasks, or just sitting with me quietly while I cried—they were all amazing, and each brought their own set of skills, personality, and beauty to the equation. I will forever remain grateful for their unwavering support, even in the midst of their own personal grieving. I couldn't have imagined a truer, more solid foundation of support. This is the gold that makes life worth living. And if any of them are reading this, please know, I didn't forget what you did for me, just because I didn't write about it here. Much of it is too personal, sacred, and close to my heart to even write about, as I would never do it justice.

LESLEY

> *Only one mountain can know the core of another mountain.*
> —*Frida Kahlo*

I posted about the accident on Facebook. It was such a painful announcement, and the act of typing it out and making the information public made it seem more real somehow. At the same time I was grateful beyond measure that I could hide privately behind my computer screen, and didn't have to notify people individually. Just making one awful, public post was enough, and it was done. The cat was out of the bag, and there was no retracting it. Comments started to pour in. I was wrapped in the sympathy of the world, while at the same time I just wanted to hide under the bed and never face another soul again.

I've never felt so lonely. I was surrounded by people and love, yet I still felt completely isolated and alone. I often found myself censoring the horror of my grief when talking to my family, to protect them, because they were also dealing with their own pain and grief. The thought of adding my pain to their burden of grief was too much, so I often found myself chained to silence.

Enter Lesley.

My friend Lesley had lost her husband, John, a few years before, in a very different but also similar way. Different in circumstances, but similar in that he was a beautiful man and absolutely the love of her life. The three of us, Lesley, Mike, and myself, had all traveled to Africa together a few years before Mike's accident, so she *knew* Mike, and we shared lots of good memories together.

Lesley wrote a comment in response to my Facebook post about how devastated she was at the news, and also that she was available to talk with, day or night. I felt connected with her and inspired to reach out.

One dark day, about a week after the funeral, I found myself alone. It was rare for me to be alone these days, as my family constantly kept company. But on that day, my sister and mom were away from my house for a couple of hours, so I took the opportunity and called Lesley.

The thing I remember most from that conversation was her underlying wisdom—authentic, pure, and solid as a rock—since she had already lived through a searing tragedy and loss herself. This common experience connected us with a golden thread, and I felt she could understand what I was going through at a level few could. It gave me some ground to stand on, and for a few moments I felt slightly less lonely.

I remember telling Lesley everything. For two long hours I just poured my heart out over the phone. I told her about the accident, my family, the funeral home, my experience at the hospital—*everything*.

Rather than try to comfort me with words, as most people do, she met me where I was with the brutal truth. She told me with harsh honesty what I could expect moving forward. She told me that I would be walking through hell for the foreseeable future. And ironically, she showed me the ridiculous value of humor.

I told her my story about getting admitted to the hospital and the absurdity of *me* telling the *doctors* what to do, and about my staying up all night with tubes sticking out of my body like a cyborg to write the obituary. Unexpectedly to me, she actually started *laughing*. Then, before I knew it, she had *me* laughing. Egads, the horror of it all! I felt so terrible and guilty that I was actually laughing, but she was right: that particular experience in the hospital was rather comical in its absurdity. I kept glancing out the window to make sure no one was coming over to *catch me* laughing. But at the same time, the laughter was like a balm to my burning soul. I will always be grateful for that phone conversation, and that forbidden laugh. It was such a gift.

MY HORSE

> The Celts used to give a horse to the person in the community who had suffered the loss of a loved one, because they knew it would help her heal the absence and, in addition, they believed that the horse was a messenger between the two worlds.
> —*Unknown*

Sometimes people ask me how I got through the chaos and pain of the hardest days immediately following the accident. When my mind was on fire and screaming, when a flood of people descended on my house to help, when the sadness crushed my spirit like a two-ton block of concrete on my chest, and when the panic became completely overwhelming, I had just one place where I could run away to. I had one place where other people did not go. I had just one place where I could find peace. I could escape to my horse, Luna.

There was a real magic that happened when I was in my bubble with Luna. Of course, the barn itself was a refuge because it's the one physical place people would let me go and be by myself. But it was more than a physical place. Luna's energy just calmed my soul. I didn't forget about what happened, but when I was with Luna, I really had to be in the present moment. I had to focus solely on her. Finally my mind had some semblance of clarity and a place to channel its energy into something productive rather than a spinning nosedive. It was safe, peaceful, and grounded with Luna. My mind settled a bit. Distractions became muffled. Time stood still.

Put plainly, there is simply no multitasking when you are working with a thousand-pound animal. A primal level of self- preservation kicked in, and it was a total escape for my brain to focus completely and 100 percent on something else. Furthermore, Luna was peace itself. There was her warmth. Her smell. Her bright and sensitive energy. Her friendly nicker. The rhythm of her feet pounding on the earth. The rocking sensation of riding her canter. The soothing sound of her eating hay.

And there was the feeling of being needed. She *needed* me for exercise and companionship. Without sounding overly dramatic, it gave me a reason to get up in the morning.

Of course, there was some deep magic living in the fact that Mike loved Luna too, and we had ten thousand memories together, so it was a very personal connection with him as well, and there was a deep comfort in that underlying foundation.

Luna was an island of escape for my heart, mind, and soul. And without trying to define what I don't fully understand, I will just say that anyone who reads about horses in therapy work will know they have a healing power deeply engrained within them. Some say they are a bridge between the physical and spiritual dimensions of our world. I know that sounds like a bit much, but if I have ever seen magic, it's been with my horse.

THE REST OF THE STORY

Of course, we all have multiple ways of coping. In addition to the items listed above, other important things that also helped me process my grief were books, journaling, talking with others about Mike, exercise, and prayer.

Talking *about Mike* with other people was one of the most cathartic things for me. It was a way to remember him, and it warmed my heart to see others remember him.

After talking with others in grief, I soon came to realize how universal the need is to remember our loved ones. Furthermore, I think it's important to bring some awareness to the world about just how important it is that we give each other permission to talk about the ones we've lost. I think sometimes other people are reluctant to bring up the name of the deceased because they don't want to make anyone feel badly by conjuring memories or stirring that emotional pot. But I can assure you, the very last thing we want is for our loved one to be forgotten.

I still love talking about Mike and his life, and reliving some of our memories. My very wisest friends and family members know this, and we routinely share stories about Mike and all our favorite memories with him.

6
THE GIFTS: *A CONCLUSION AND A CONTINUATION OF GRIEF*

> What a pleasure it is. To know gravity.
> —*Victoria Erickson*

I am still learning to manage my grief, in all its complexity. As grief evolves, it becomes almost a living, breathing companion that continues to walk with us in life. We learn to sit with it. We learn how harvest its gifts.

Just like any noun in the English language, the word *grief* is just a marker that attempts to name ... *something*. But in this case, what is that *something* exactly?

Writing has always been a way for me to manage my thoughts. Words have real power within them. Harnessing an intangible emotion, feeling, or experience within the confines of a word, or a string of words artfully put together in a phrase or sentence, is a way to define, own, and tame it. We give shape to the shapeless. We capture it all in a box with sides and edges. The more slippery the essence of that emotion, feeling, or experience is, the more power there is in naming it.

So here we have the word *grief*. Such a short, little slip of a word for a Pandora's box of complexity.

One dictionary defines *grief* as a noun, particularly the following:

> Grief – A deep sorrow, especially that caused by someone's death.

or

> Grief – The response to loss, particularly to the loss of someone or some living thing that has died, to which a bond or affection was formed. Although conventionally focused on the emotional

response to loss, grief also has physical, cognitive, behavioral, social, cultural, spiritual and philosophical dimensions.

Yes, it is all of those things.

I think it can also be described as *a process we go through*, complicated and ever evolving.

It can be hard to evolve in our grief, because we think we are *letting go* of our loved one. To accept the loss and move forward seems almost like a betrayal of our loved one's spirit. The suffering becomes a type of home to us because it is comfortable—not pleasant but familiar. Suffering is a way to stay in the gravity of the loss, and by doing so, we mistakenly think we honor it. But perhaps there is a better way to honor it.

The early stages of grief are dense, a low vibration of energy. To not evolve in our grief is to get stuck in that lower-level energy. *And getting stuck will not allow the gifts of grief to fully emerge.*

Imagine, for a moment, that as our grief evolves, we begin to focus more on the love of the one we lost, instead of the darkness of the loss. Instead, we focus on the abundance of the love we had, and still have, for the person we lost. Love is the *highest vibration of energy* in the universe. It's light and airy and allows for movement, gratitude, and grace. Imagine we focus on *that*.

Perhaps that shift in focus will still allow us a real connection with the person we lost, whereas the darkness of early grief could cloak, dampen, and cloud that connection. For example, I never considered talking to Mike after the accident, until I started to do it. I couldn't imagine a world where his spirit just disappeared, until I considered it hadn't. I couldn't be grateful for anything, until I started to focus on the beautiful parts of our story (and there were many) and until I allowed myself to evolve to that place of awareness. Eventually, slowly, I started to let go of the darkness, but I didn't let go of the light or the love. Instead I leaned into the *love*.

It's easy to be angry and resentful. It's easy to despair and stagnate in the darkness. But to get stuck in the lower stages of grief is to get lost in the darkness of the tunnel, where we despair and cannot help ourselves, let alone anyone else. To evolve into the higher stages of grief is to evolve into our new identity. We will never be the same, but we can be better. We can own the deeper self we found in that dark tunnel and bring that new, deeper self into the light. We have new gifts now!

What are they? you may ask. I suppose each person may find different gifts, but I believe some of them are likely universal. Here were some of my gifts.

Light

There's a new lightness we can bring to our living. Life isn't all the serious business we make of it.

Strength

We are more fragile in some ways, but strong as steel in others. Both are gifts.

Relativity

Is that flat tire on the car really a big deal? Even the job loss, the financial crisis, or the illness? Yes, some issues might still be serious. But the gift in big loss is that our entire scale has shifted, and even big concerns lose some gravity.

Priorities

It's easier to say no to things that don't matter, and that makes space for saying yes to the things that do.

It's a little less urgent to have a perfectly clean kitchen and a little more important to make those cookies with the kids.

The dishes can wait, but the after-dinner conversation with loved ones cannot.

Joy

Ironically, it's easier to smile and laugh now.

Grace

It's easier to see the light in other humans, and to forgive their shortcomings. Give grace to everyone. Let's just assume each person is doing their best.

The truth is, we are all evolving in some way or another. To refuse to forgive someone is to hold them hostage to a previous version of themselves. (That goes for how we forgive ourselves too.)

Happiness

A simple walk outside on an airy spring day with green grass under your bare feet and warm sunshine on your shoulders feels as good as accomplishing a traditional lifetime goal of big success, money, or prestige.

Service

Helping others becomes the most healing balm in the universe.

Kindness

Kindness becomes our compass. It rises above the density of human ego and governs our actions.

Humility

Humility becomes part of our core. It's okay not to understand everything, but the key is knowing there is much we don't know.

Love

We learn to focus on the love. The early stages of grief separate us from love. The evolved stages of grief reveal it, strengthen it, and connect us more fully with it.

Healing

And last, but not least, we can sit with each other in grief. We will all have great loss in our lives. We can help others through the tunnel because we have been there. At the very least, we can sit with them in the dark, so they know they aren't alone, until they find their light.

> Though my soul may set in darkness,
> it will rise in perfect light;
> I have loved the stars too fondly to
> be fearful of the night.
> —"The Old Astronomer,"
> Sarah Williams

Michael Alan Anderson

1973-2016

CPSIA information can be obtained
at www.ICGtesting.com
Printed in the USA
BVHW032201050323
659759BV00008B/48